HOW CAN I MAKE EARTH DAY EVERYDAY?

a kid's guide to a healthy planet

Vea Lewis

copyright **2022** by seven monkeys publishing
all rights reserved. this book or any portion thereof
may not be reproduced or used in any manner whatsoever
without the express written permision of the publisher
except for the use of brief quotations in a book review.

ISBN: **9798437374207**

printed in the united states of america
first printing, 2022
seven monkeys publishing

Everyone **LOVES** Earth. It is our **HOME.**

Keeping the Earth clean and healthy is a BIG job.

Would you believe me
if I told you kids can help
keep the Earth healthy?
If every kid does one
or two things to help
the Earth it will
add up and make a
BIG difference.

Did you know that trees
take **YEARS** to grow
big and strong?
You can help the
Earth by planting saplings.
Every tree planted helps
the Earth by replacing
trees cut down by
people around the world.

A sapling is a baby tree.

Earth loves her birds
and you should, too!
A great way to help
the birds is to make a
birdfeeder. Just remember to
keep it full. The birds will
thank you!

Look up online what your local birds eat
to make your feeder extra popular.

Bees and other pollinators
don't just help flowers grow.
They also help our food grow!
We need them, but right now
they need US, too.
Kids can help pollinators
like bees and butterflies
by planting wildflower
seeds in their town.

There are over **200,000** species
that pollinate plants.

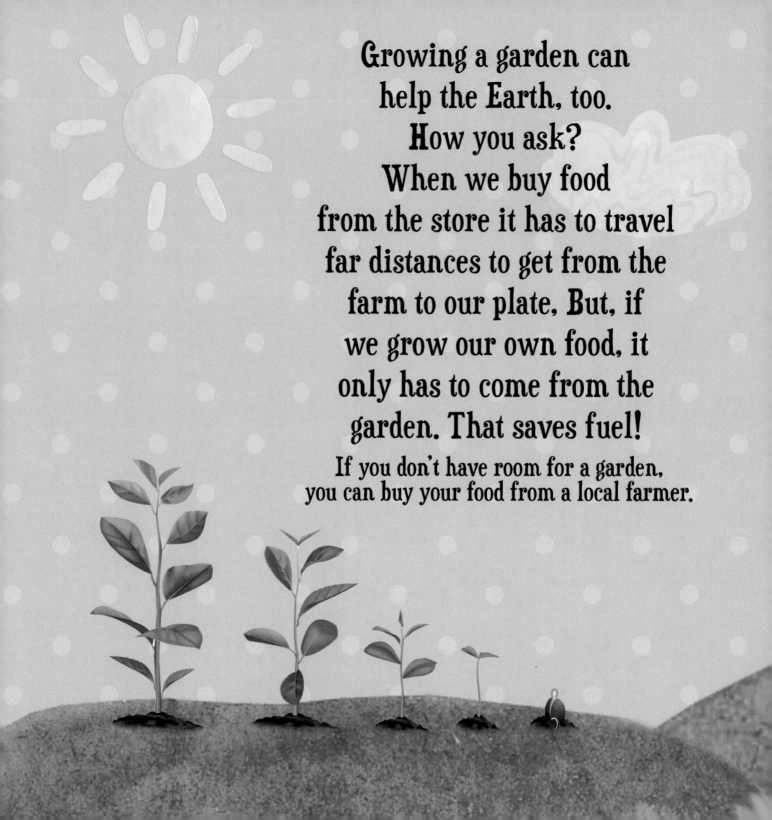

Growing a garden can
help the Earth, too.
How you ask?
When we buy food
from the store it has to travel
far distances to get from the
farm to our plate. But, if
we grow our own food, it
only has to come from the
garden. That saves fuel!

If you don't have room for a garden,
you can buy your food from a local farmer.

What should we do
with our cans and bottles?
If we throw them in the
garbage, they end up in
a landfill.

The answer is EASY!
You should RECYCLE them!

But even better than RECYCLING is REUSING!

Why?
1. Recycling takes energy. Reusing doesn't.
2. It causes less pollution.
3. You choose what the item becomes.
4. Reusing helps you flex your creativity!

Reuse

Want to start reusing today?
You can refill your water
bottle instead of recycling it.

Some people don't treat the Earth with respect, They leave their garbage on the ground. This is called littering.

You can help the Earth
by setting up a clean-up day.

National Clean Up Day is
the 3rd Saturday in September.

What about your garbage?

Food waste is amazing!

It can be turned back into the
dirt that it came from.
When food waste is layered in
between twigs and yard clippings,
it can turn into compost in
as fast as **6-8 weeks.**

Imagine how happy and healthy your garden will be with fresh compost!

Are there ways you can help the Earth while inside your home?

REDUCING how much you waste energy and resources can make a BIG difference.

To save energy and cause less pollution, you should turn off lights and electronics when you aren't using them.

Less than 1 percent of the world's water is drinking water. Turning off the water when you aren't using it is a way to not waste it!

Another way to **REDUCE** your
energy use is to play with
different toys.

Look for toys in your house that don't
need batteries or to be plugged into the wall.

The only energy these toys need is...

KID ENERGY!

Working hard to keep the planet
healthy is important.
But, it is also important to
enjoy the clean planet.
Get outside and have fun!

What else can you do?

You can tell everyone you know
how they can help the Earth, too.

The most important thing
to remember is that
you can help the Earth every day.
Earth is the only planet we call home.
Reducing, reusing, recycling
are our way to give the Earth a

GREAT BIG HUG!

Earth Day activities

1. Clean up your neighborhood.

2. Make a birdfeeder with a pine cone, peanut butter, seeds, and string.

3. Start a garden. You can grow food or wildflowers.

4. Have a nature scavenger hunt.

5. Plant a sapling. Baby trees need time to grow. Measure your tree's growth every month.

6. Go for a family bike ride or walk.

7. Turn off the TV and read a book.

8. Make and decorate a reusable tote bag. You can even make bags out of old tee shirts.

9. Watch nature videos on youtube, and learn more about how to help our animal friends.

10. Visit VeaLewis.com for more FREE games and printables!

Made in the USA
Middletown, DE
22 April 2023

29306507R00020